A WORLD OF RECIPES

Mexico

REVISED AND UPDATED

Julie McCulloch

Heinemann Library
Chicago, Illinois

www.heinemannraintree.com
Visit our website to find out
more information about
Heinemann-Raintree books.

To order:

☎ Phone 888-454-2279

💻 Visit www.heinemannraintree.com
to browse our catalog and order online.

© 2001, 2009 Heinemann Library
an imprint of Capstone Global Library, LLC
Chicago, Illinois

Edited by David Andrews and Diyan Leake
Designed by Richard Parker
Illustrated by Nicholas Beresford-Davis
Picture research by Mica Brancic
Printed and bound in China by Leo Paper Products Ltd

13 12 11 10 09
10 9 8 7 6 5 4 3 2 1

New edition ISBN: 978-1-4329-2230-6

**The Library of Congress has cataloged the first edition
as follows:**
McCulloch, Julie, 1973-.
  Mexico/Julie McCulloch.
    p. cm. -- (A world of recipes)
  Includes bibliographical references and index.
  ISBN 978-1-58810-088-7 (HC) 978-1-58810-390-1(PB)
            Cookery, Mexican—Juvenile literature. 2.
Cookery—Mexico—Juvenile literature. [1. Cookery, Mexican.
2.Mexico–Social life and customs.] I. Title.
TX716.M4 M393 2001
641.5972—dc22   00-059743

Acknowledgments

The author and publishers are grateful to the following for
permission to reproduce copyright material: © Capstone
Global Library Ltd/MM Studios pp. 16, 17; Gareth Boden
pp. 8–15, 18–43; Getty Images (National Geographic/©
Gina Martin) p. 7; © Getty Images p. 5 (Taxi/Ty Allison);
Photolibrary Group p. 6 (© SGM SGM).

Cover photograph of tortillas and salsa reproduced with
permission of Getty Images (Photographer's Choice/Justin
Lightley).

Every effort has been made to contact copyright holders of
any material reproduced in this book. Any omissions will
be rectified in subsequent printings if notice is given to the
publisher.

All the Internet addresses (URLs) given in this book were valid
at the time of going to press. However, due to the dynamic
nature of the Internet, some addresses may have changed, or
sites may have changed or ceased to exist since publication.
While the author and Publishers regret any inconvenience this
may cause readers, no responsibility for any such changes can
be accepted by either the author or the Publishers.

Contents

Key: *easy **medium ***difficult

Mexico 4

Mexican Food 6

Ingredients 8

Before You Start 10

Tortillas .... 12 **

Guacamole .... 14 *

Cornbread .... 16 **

Corn Soup .... 18 **

Broiled Corn on the Cob with Salsa .... 20 **

Cheese-Filled Enchiladas .... 22 ***

Bean and Potato Patties .... 24 ***

Picadillo .... 26 **

Chili con Carne .... 28 **

Fish Burritos .... 30 ***

Mexican Rice .... 32 **

Savory Fruit Salad .... 34 *

Rice Pudding .... 36 **

Cinnamon Oranges ....38 *

Caramel Custard .... 40 ***

Mexican Hot Chocolate .... 42 **

Further Information 44

Healthy Eating 45

Glossary 46

Index 48

Some words are shown in bold, **like this**. You can find out what they mean by looking in the glossary.

Mexico

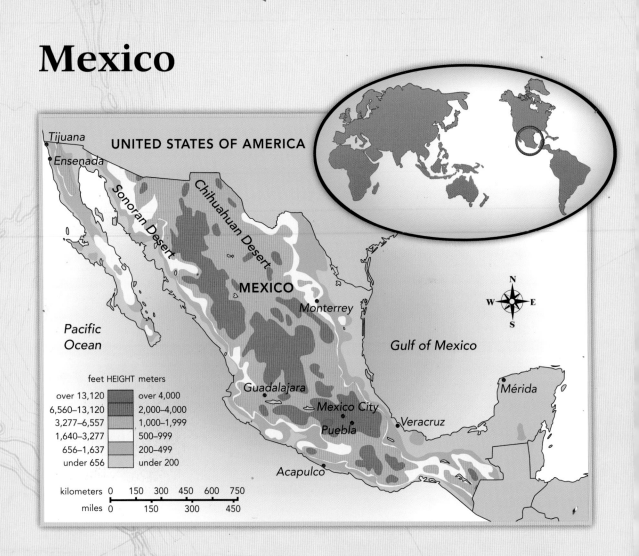

The Republic of Mexico is the eighth largest nation in the world. Mexico has long coastlines on the Pacific Ocean and the Gulf of Mexico. The Sonoran and the Chihuahuan deserts are in the far north. The northern plain, with rolling hills, is home to ranches and farms. The central mountain ranges feature two active volcanoes. Southern Mexico contains flat, marshy land and rain forests.

The climate of Mexico is also diverse. The south is hot and wet, while the north has a milder, drier climate. There may even be snow on the mountain. The weather on the coasts is hot and sometimes humid.

In the past

The Mayans were people who lived in Mexico from 600 to 900 CE. They grew sweet corn, beans, and squash.

Mayan culture was based on religion, with many festivals for the gods. The Mayans built temples shaped like pyramids. Science, mathematics, and astronomy were also important.

The Aztec people (900–1500 CE) came from the north. They created a rich, powerful **empire**. Their capital city was filled with markets, temples, and floating gardens. This city eventually became Mexico City, the modern capital. An Aztec legend about an eagle eating a snake is shown by an emblem on the Mexican flag.

In the early 16th century, Mexico was conquered by Spain and became known as "New Spain." It remained under Spanish rule until its war of independence began in 1810. Spanish is still the main language spoken in Mexico. The citizens of Mexico are mainly *mestizos* (a mixture of Spanish and native peoples).

Mexico today

Today, the Roman Catholic religion and family life are important in Mexico. The many holidays include saints' days, when there are church services, parades, fireworks, dancing, and feasting. The Day of the Dead is celebrated after Halloween. It is a time for families to remember loved ones.

At Christmas parties, children break open *piñatas* filled with sweets or toys. Families dress up as Biblical characters and sing carols. Mexicans also celebrate Independence Day. Popular sports throughout the year are bullfighting and soccer.

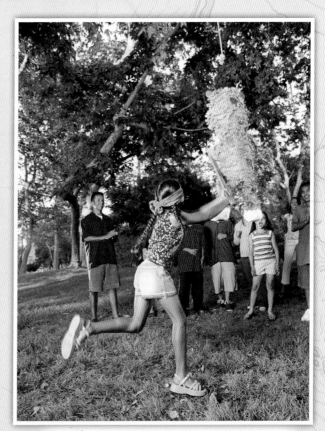

↑ *Piñatas* are a fun part of Mexican Christmas celebrations.

Mexican Food

Farming has existed in Mexico for over 7,000 years. Once maize began to be planted, early tribes abandoned a **nomadic** hunter-gatherer lifestyle and settled in villages. The Mayans and Aztecs also grew squash, beans, tomatoes, and chili peppers.

The Spanish introduced European foods, including milk, cheese, chicken, and wheat. Ancient foods and Spanish foods blended to create modern Mexican cooking, with its bright colors. Many different vegetables and fruits are used, while chilies add spiciness. Maize remains important for making tortillas and tamales (flat breads). Tomatoes and beans are used in stews and soups.

Around the country

Mexico's geography allows a variety of food to be produced. On the northern plains, beef cattle are raised. A wide array of vegetables grow in the cool central mountains.

↑ These pineapples are growing on a plantation in a hot, tropical climate.

The hotter areas in the south produce **tropical** fruits such as papayas, pineapples, and coconuts. Rice is grown extensively in the southeast, with its **monsoon**-type rains. Two crops a year are possible. Most Mexican meals feature a rice dish, either savory or sweet. Seafood is abundant along the coastlines.

Markets have been an important part of life for centuries. In Aztec markets, cocoa beans were used as payment. Today, towns often have street markets where Mexicans can meet friends and buy their traditional food.

Mexican meals

At breakfast, many Mexicans have coffee with cinnamon and sugar, sweet rolls, and maybe yogurt. Lunch, or *comida*, is usually the main meal. It often consists of three courses: a starter, a main course, and a dessert.

The early evening meal—*merienda*—is usually a light snack such as cereal, tortillas, and hot chocolate. The day ends with *cena*, a light supper, which can be leftovers from *comida*, a potato and onion omelette, or a sandwich.

Festival foods

Special foods are important at festivals. Fruit drinks are given out by schools and businesses during Lent, the 40 days before Easter. During Holy Week (Easter week), ice cream and fruit bars are sold from pushcarts. One summer fiesta celebrates the vanilla bean.

The Day of the Dead features bread shaped like dogs, sugar skulls, and chocolate coffins. On this day, people gather in cemeteries for a picnic. To celebrate Independence Day, Mexicans eat green chilies stuffed with meat and spices. Before Christmas, neighbors throw *posadas*, or parties.

↑ A wide variety of chilies can be found in the markets of Mexico.

Ingredients

peppers

avocados

tomatoes

beans

sweet corn

tortillas

chocolate

chilies

The ingredients for most Mexican dishes are quite easy to find in supermarkets. Here are some of the most common ones.

Avocados

Avocados originally came from Central and South America. The word *avocado* comes from the Mexican word *ahuacatl*. Avocados are a fruit, not a vegetable, and they have a very large pit in the center.

Beans

Different beans are used in many Mexican recipes. Two of the most common types of beans are lima beans (used in the recipe on page 24) and kidney beans (used in the recipe on page 28). They are easiest to use if you buy them in cans.

Chilies

Chilies are spicy peppers used in many Mexican dishes. There are hundreds of different kinds—some are quite mild, and others are very, very hot! Fresh chilies contain an oil that can make your eyes and skin sting if it touches them, so it is a good idea to use chili powder, made from ground-up dried chilies, rather than fresh ones. If you don't like spicy food, just leave out the chili powder.

Chocolate

Chocolate has been eaten and drunk in Mexico for thousands of years. It is made from the roasted, crushed beans of the cocoa plant. In Mexico, chocolate is made into hot drinks, used in desserts, and used in savory sauces. Plain, dark chocolate is the best kind to use in Mexican recipes.

Sweet corn

Sweet corn was one of the first plants grown in Mexico, and it is used in many dishes. You can buy sweet corn fresh on the cob (either in its leafy case or with this stripped off), frozen on the cob, or separated from the cob (frozen or canned).

Tomatoes

Tomatoes are used in many Mexican recipes. You can use either fresh or canned tomatoes for the recipes in this book.

Tortillas

Tortillas are flat circles of bread. They are eaten with many different meals in Mexico. Two different types of tortillas are eaten in Mexico—wheat tortillas (which contain wheat flour) and corn tortillas (which contain flour made from ground sweet corn). Sweet corn flour can be difficult to find, so the recipe for tortillas in this book is for wheat tortillas.

Before You Start

Which recipe should I try?

The recipes you choose to make depend on many things. Some recipes make a good main course, while others are better as starters. Some are easy, while others are more difficult.

The top right-hand page of each recipe has information that can help you. It tells you how long each recipe will take and how many people it serves. You can multiply or divide the quantities if you want to cook for more or fewer people. This section also shows how difficult each dish is to make: the recipes are easy (*), medium (**), or difficult (***) to cook. The symbols in the corner can help you quickly find certain recipes. Here is a key that will help you.

Healthy choice: These recipes are healthy to eat.

Quick and easy: These recipes are quick and easy to make.

Sweet treat: These recipes make a good dessert or sweet snack.

This symbol ⚠ is a sign of a dangerous step in a recipe. For these steps, be extra careful or ask an adult to help.

Kitchen rules

There are a few basic rules you should always follow when you cook:

- Ask an adult if you can use the kitchen.
- Wash your hands before you start.
- Wear an apron to protect your clothes. Tie back long hair.
- Be very careful when using sharp knives.
- Never leave pan handles sticking out—it could be dangerous if you bump into them.
- Always wear oven mitts to lift things in and out of the oven.
- Wash fruits and vegetables before you use them.

Quantities and measurements

Ingredients for recipes can be measured in two different ways. Imperial measurements use cups, pounds, ounces, and fluid ounces. Metric measurements use grams, liters, and milliliters. In the recipes in this book you will see the following abbreviations:

tbsp = tablespoons	oz. = ounces	cm = centimeters
tsp = teaspoons	g = grams	ml = milliliters
lbs = pounds	in. = inches	

Utensils

To cook the recipes in this book, you will need these utensils, as well as kitchen essentials such as forks, spoons, plates, and bowls.

- Baking pan
- Baking sheet
- Chopping board
- Foil
- Food processor or blender
- Frying pan
- Grater
- Large, flat, ovenproof dish
- Heatproof bowl
- Kitchen scale
- Measuring cup (for liquids)
- Measuring cups (for dry ingredients) and measuring spoons
- Potato masher
- Rolling pin
- Saucepan with lid
- Sharp knife
- Sieve or **colander**
- Whisk
- Wooden toothpicks

Tortillas

Tortillas are eaten with many Mexican meals. Sometimes they are served as an accompaniment to the meal, but often they form part of the meal itself, usually by being wrapped around different fillings.

The recipes for cheese-filled enchiladas (page 22) and fish burritos (page 30) use tortillas, so you will need to make some tortillas before cooking these dishes. You can also buy ready-made tortillas, but here is how to make your own.

What You need

1 cup all-purpose flour (+ a few extra tbsp to sprinkle on the chopping board)

1 tsp salt

2 tbsp olive oil

4 tbsp warm water

What You do

 1 Put the flour and salt into a mixing bowl. Mix in the oil with a spoon, then gradually stir in the warm water until the mixture starts to form a **dough**.

 2 **Sprinkle** some flour onto a chopping board. **Knead** the dough on the board until it is smooth.

 3 Divide the dough into four pieces, to make four tortillas.

 4 Shape one piece of dough into a ball, then flatten it.

 5 Sprinkle some more flour onto the board and onto a rolling pin. Roll out the ball of dough into a circle, until the dough is as thin as you can make it without breaking it.

6 Heat a frying pan until it sizzles when you sprinkle a drop of water into it. Put the tortilla into the pan.

 7 Cook the tortilla for one minute, then turn it over and cook the other side for 30 seconds. Slide the cooked tortilla out of the pan onto a plate.

8 Repeat steps 4 to 7 with the other three pieces of dough.

STORING TORTILLAS

You can store your tortillas to use later. Put a square of waxed paper between each tortilla so that they do not stick together. Leave them to **cool**, then put the stack of tortillas into a plastic bag. They will keep for several days in the refrigerator.

Guacamole

Guacamole is eaten all over Mexico. It can be eaten as a snack, spread on tortillas, or used as an accompaniment to other dishes.

What you need

- 1 onion
- A handful of fresh cilantro leaves (see box on next page)
- ¼ tsp chili powder (optional)
- 1 avocado
- 1 tbsp lemon juice

What you do

 1. **Peel** the skin from the onion and finely **chop** half of it.

 2. Finely chop the fresh cilantro.

 3. In a bowl, mix together the chopped onion, cilantro, and chili powder (if you are using it).

4. Cut the avocado in half lengthways. Use a spoon to remove the pit.

5. Use the spoon to scoop out the flesh of the avocado into the bowl, leaving the skin behind.

 6. Add the lemon juice to the mixture.

 7. **Mash** all the ingredients together with a fork.

CILANTRO

Cilantro is an herb that looks a bit like parsley.
It is used a lot in Mexican cooking. You will usually
find fresh cilantro in the fruits and vegetables section
of supermarkets. Cilantro has a unique flavor that is
associated with Mexican food, so try to track it down if
you can. However, If you cannot find any, try using fresh
parsley leaves instead.

Cornbread

Mexican cornbread is a sweet-tasting bread that is easy to make. It is often served at meal times in Mexican households. The bread gets its name from the cornmeal that is used as one of the primary ingredients in making it. Other flours made from maize, such as polenta, can also be used to make cornbread, although it will not taste quite like the real thing.

What You need

1 cup all-purpose flour

1 cup fine cornmeal or polenta

1 tbsp baking powder

½ tsp salt

2 eggs

1¼ cups 2 percent milk

3½ tbsp butter

1 cup canned sweet corn

¼ tsp chili powder (optional)

What You do

1 Lightly **grease** a baking pan.

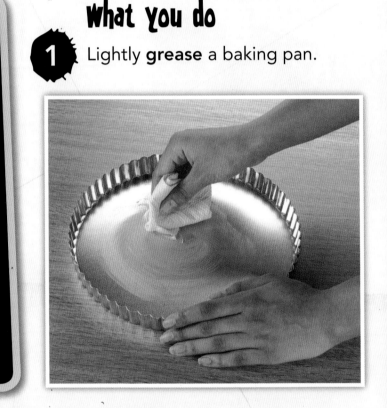

2 **Preheat** the oven to 400°F (200°C).

3 Combine the flour, cornmeal or polenta, baking powder, and salt in a mixing bowl.

4 **Beat** the eggs with the milk in another bowl.

5 **Melt** the butter and add it to the eggs and milk.

Drain and rinse the sweet corn and mix it with the eggs, along with the chili powder, if using. Add the egg mixture to the dry ingredients and stir to a smooth batter.

 Pour the mixture into the prepared pan. **Bake** for 20 to 25 minutes until it is golden brown, firm, and beginning to pull away from the sides of the pan.

8 Cut it into pieces while still warm and serve right away.

Corn Soup

Hot soup is often served in the cold, mountainous regions of Mexico. Most lunches start with a bowl of soup, and many evening meals consist of soup served with a stack of tortillas. This simple corn soup is full of flavor and is very **nourishing**.

If you use the frozen sweet corn, you need to **thaw** it before you use it. You can do this in two ways:

a) Take it out of the freezer at least an hour before you want to use it, and leave it to stand;

b) Pour hot water over the sweet corn, leave it to stand for a couple of minutes, then carefully empty the sweet corn into a **colander** or sieve to **drain**.

What you need

- 1 onion
- 1 red pepper
- 2 cups water
- 1 tbsp sunflower oil
- 1 cup canned or frozen sweet corn
- 1 vegetable stock cube
- ½ cup plain natural yogurt

What you do

 1 **Peel** the skin from the onion and finely **chop** half of it.

 2 Cut the red pepper in half, then scoop out the seeds. Chop half of the flesh into strips.

3 Put the water into a saucepan and bring it to a **boil**. Crumble the stock cube into the water and stir until it **dissolves**. Put the stock to one side.

 4 Heat the oil in a saucepan. **Fry** the chopped onion and red pepper for about five minutes.

 5 Put the onion and pepper mixture and the sweet corn into a blender or food processor. **Blend** until smooth.

6 Put the mixture back into the saucepan and add the stock.

7 **Simmer** the soup for about five minutes, until it is hot.

8 Stir in the yogurt. You can use the other half of the red pepper to **garnish** your soup.

COLD SOUP
This dish can also be served cold for a refreshing summer soup. Let the soup **cool**, then put it into the refrigerator for a couple of hours before serving it.

Broiled Corn on the Cob with Salsa

Corn on the cob can be eaten on its own or with a sauce. This recipe shows you how to make corn on the cob with salsa, which is a spicy Mexican sauce made with tomatoes and fruit. Mexican people eat salsa with many different dishes. In Mexican restaurants, you often find a bowl of salsa on the table along with the salt and pepper.

What you need

- 1 onion
- 2 tomatoes
- 1 red pepper
- 1 slice of canned pineapple
- 2 cobs of sweet corn
- 2 tbsp sunflower oil
- 2 tsp chili powder (optional)

What you do

1 **Peel** the onion and finely **chop** half of it.

2 Chop the tomatoes into small pieces.

3 Cut the red pepper in half, then scoop the seeds out. Chop half of the flesh into strips.

4 Chop the slice of pineapple into small pieces.

 5 Heat 1 tbsp of the oil in a saucepan over medium heat. Add the chopped onion and the chili powder (if you are using any). **Fry** for five minutes, or until the onion is soft.

6 Add the chopped tomatoes, red pepper, and pineapple. Turn the heat down to low and **cover** the pan. Leave the salsa to **simmer** for about 10 minutes, stirring occasionally.

While the salsa is cooking, brush the remaining 1 tbsp of oil onto the sweet corn.

 Put the sweet corn cobs on a baking sheet and **broil** them for about 10 minutes, turning them occasionally so they are cooked on all sides.

Put the sweet corn onto plates, and spoon half of the salsa sauce onto each plate.

HOT AND SALTY

For a really quick snack, try making corn on the cob with butter and salt. Broil the sweet corn as described above, then spread butter on them while they are still hot, so it **melts** into the corn. **Sprinkle** them with salt and eat them right away. Be careful they don't burn the inside of your mouth, though!

Cheese-Filled Enchiladas

Enchiladas are tortillas rolled around a filling. These cheesy enchiladas are served with a hot tomato sauce.

What You need

For the tomato sauce:
1 onion
1 clove of garlic
1 cup tomatoes
1 tbsp sunflower oil
For the filling:
1 cup half-fat hard cheese (for example, Cheddar)
1 cup cottage cheese

4 tortillas (bought or homemade—see pages 12–13)

What You do

 Preheat the oven to 375°F (190°C).

 Peel the onion and the garlic and finely **chop** them.

 Chop the tomatoes into small pieces.

 Heat the oil in a frying pan. **Fry** the onion and garlic on low heat for five minutes, or until the onion is soft, but not brown.

5 Add the chopped tomatoes. **Cover** the pan and **simmer** the mixture for about 20 minutes, stirring occasionally.

DIFFERENT FILLINGS
You can make enchiladas with all sorts of different fillings. Here are some ideas:
- Guacamole (see page 14)
- Picadillo (see page 26)
- Chili con carne (see page 28)

6 While the tomato sauce is simmering, **grate** the cheese. Mix ⅔ of the cheese with all of the cottage cheese in a bowl. (Keep the rest of the cheese for later.)

 7 Place 2 tbsp of the cheese mixture onto each tortilla, then roll it into a tube.

8 Put the rolled-up tortillas into a large, flat, ovenproof dish.

9 Pour the tomato sauce over the rolled-up tortillas, then **sprinkle** the remaining cheese over the top.

10 Cover the dish with foil and **bake** in the oven for 30 minutes. Remove the foil and bake for another 15 minutes, until the cheese is brown and bubbling.

Bean and Potato Patties

Beans are eaten in many different ways in Mexico. These bean and potato patties are good served with spicy salsa (see recipe on page 20).

What you need

- 1 medium potato
- ½ cup half-fat hard cheese (for example, Cheddar)
- 1 egg
- ½ cup canned lima beans
- 2 tbsp flour
- ½ tbsp sunflower oil

What you do

 1 Carefully **peel** the potatoes using a sharp knife, then cut them into small pieces.

 2 Put the potatoes into a saucepan full of water and **boil** them for about 15 minutes, until they are soft.

 3 While the potatoes are boiling, **grate** the cheese into a small bowl.

 4 Crack the egg into a bowl. **Beat** it with a fork or a whisk until the yolk and the white are mixed.

 5 When the potatoes are soft, **drain** them by emptying the pan into a **colander** or sieve. Put the drained potatoes back into the pan.

 6 Drain the lima beans and put them into the pan with the potatoes. **Mash** the potatoes and beans together with a fork or a potato masher.

 7 Add the grated cheese and beaten egg to the mashed potatoes and beans. Mix everything together well.

 8 Divide the mixture into four pieces, and shape each piece into a flattened round patty.

9 **Sprinkle** the flour onto a chopping board. Turn the patties over a couple of times on the board to coat them in flour.

10 Heat the oil in a frying pan over low heat. Put the patties into the pan and **fry** them gently for 10 minutes. Turn them over carefully, and fry on the other side for another 10 minutes.

Picadillo

Picadillo is a main course dish made from ground beef, fruit, and spices. It is usually served with long-grain rice or tortillas.

What you need

½ onion
1 clove of garlic
1 apple
1 tbsp sunflower oil
1 cup tomatoes
7 oz. ground beef
¼ tsp chili powder
    (optional)
¼ cup raisins
½ tsp cinnamon
½ tsp cumin

What you do

 1 **Peel** the onion and the garlic and **chop** them finely.

2 Using a sharp knife, carefully cut the apple into pieces. Don't use the core of the apple.

3 Chop the tomatoes into small pieces.

4 Heat the oil in a frying pan over medium heat. Add the ground beef, the onion, and the garlic.

5 **Fry** the mixture for 15 minutes, stirring occasionally, until the onion is soft and the beef is brown.

Add the apple, tomatoes, chili powder (if using any), raisins, cinnamon, and cumin to the pan.

 Cover the pan and cook the picadillo over low heat for about 15 minutes, stirring occasionally.

PICADILLO-STUFFED PEPPERS

Picadillo is sometimes served stuffed into red peppers. This looks impressive, but is easy to do! Carefully cut the top off a red pepper and scoop out the seeds. Spoon the cooked picadillo into the hollow pepper, replace the pepper's top, and **bake** in an oven at 350°F (180°C) for about 40 minutes.

Chili con Carne

Chili con carne means "chili with meat." Chilies are an important part of many Mexican dishes. In the past, Mexican people believed that chilies could cure many illnesses, including toothaches and earaches. Modern science has proved that chilies do contain lots of healthy **vitamins**. Serve chili con carne with long-grain rice.

What you need

1 tbsp sunflower oil

7 oz. lean ground beef

1 onion

1 clove of garlic

½ tsp chili powder (optional)

1 cup tomatoes

⅓ cup canned kidney beans

What you do

1 **Preheat** the oven to 325°F (160°C).

2 **Peel** the skin from the onion and the garlic clove and finely **chop** them.

3 Chop the tomatoes into small pieces.

4 Heat the oil in a frying pan over medium heat. Add the chopped onion, garlic, and ground beef.

5 **Fry** the mixture for about 15 minutes, stirring occasionally to stop it from sticking.

6 Add the chili powder (if you are using any), chopped tomatoes, and **drained** kidney beans to the pan.

7 Cook the mixture for another five minutes, then pour it carefully into an ovenproof dish.

 8 **Cover** the dish and cook your chili con carne in the oven for one hour.

 9 Put the cooked chili in a serving bowl. You can also serve chili with tortillas.

VEGETARIAN CHILI

You can make a **vegetarian** version of this dish, called *chili sin carne*—"chili without meat"! Just replace the ground beef with chopped vegetables such as zucchini, mushrooms, and red peppers.

Fish Burritos

These are little packages of fish, wrapped in tortillas. They are delicious served with guacamole (see recipe on page 14). You can use fresh or frozen fish for this recipe, but make sure frozen fish is well **thawed**.

What you need

For the filling:

1 onion

2 fish fillets (thawed if frozen)

½ tbsp sunflower oil

¼ tsp chili powder (optional)

¼ cup plain natural yogurt

4 tortillas (bought or homemade—see pages 12–13)

½ cup half-fat hard cheese (for example, Cheddar)

What you do

 Preheat the oven to 350°F (180°C).

 Peel the onion and finely **chop** half of it.

 Put the fish into a saucepan. Just cover it with water, bring to a **boil**, and then **simmer** for five minutes.

 Drain the water from the fish. Use a fork to **flake** it into a bowl, making sure you take out the skin and any bones.

⚠ 5 Heat the oil in a frying pan over medium heat. **Fry** the chopped onion and chili powder (if you are using any) for five minutes, until the onion is soft. Add this mixture to the fish.

6 Add the yogurt to the fish and onions and mix well.

 7 Put a couple of spoonfuls of the fish mixture onto each tortilla, then fold the tortilla. Insert toothpicks through each burrito to keep it closed.

 8 Put the burritos into an ovenproof dish.

9 **Grate** the cheese over the burritos. **Cover** the dish with foil and **bake** for 30 minutes.

10 Remove the toothpicks before serving.

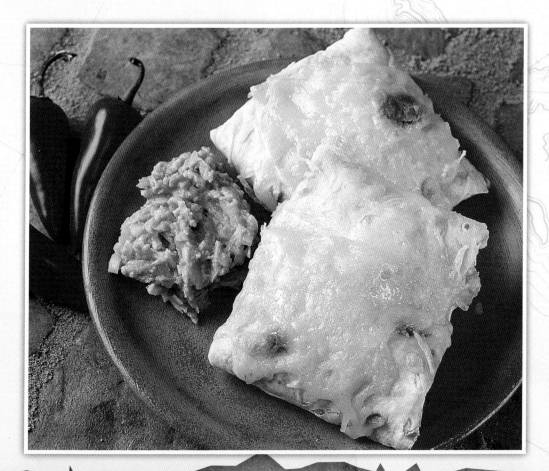

Mexican Rice

This rice dish is **nourishing** enough to serve as a main course on its own. There are two different types of rice—long and short grain. This dish works best made with long-grain rice.

What you need

- ½ onion
- 1 clove of garlic
- 1 cup tomatoes
- 1¼ cups water
- 1 vegetable stock cube
- 1 tbsp sunflower oil
- ¾ cup rice
- ½ tsp chili powder (optional)
- ½ cup frozen peas

What you do

 1 **Peel** the onion and garlic and finely **chop** them.

 2 Chop the tomatoes into small pieces.

 3 Put the water into a saucepan and bring it to a **boil**. Crumble the stock cube into the water and stir until it **dissolves**. Put the stock to one side.

 4 Heat the oil in a saucepan over medium heat. Add the onions, garlic, and rice, and cook for five minutes, stirring all the time to stop the rice from sticking.

5 Add the tomatoes, stock, chili powder (if you are using any), and peas to the pan. Bring to a boil, then reduce the heat to low.

 6 **Cover** the pan and **simmer** for about 20 minutes, stirring occasionally, until all the liquid has been soaked up.

HEALTHY EXTRAS

In some regions of Mexico, rice and beans are eaten at nearly every meal. Rice and beans are both cheap ingredients that provide a great deal of nourishment—**protein** from the beans and **carbohydrates** from the rice.

Savory Fruit Salad

You can serve this salad with many of the dishes in this book. It goes well with meat dishes such as picadillo and chili con carne.

What you need

- 1 small head of lettuce
- 1 carrot
- 1 apple
- 2 slices of canned pineapple
- 1 banana
- 1 orange
- 2 tbsp lemon juice
- 2 tbsp sunflower oil

What you do

 Cut or the **shred** the lettuce leaves and put them into a salad bowl.

 Carefully wash the carrot and **grate** it into the salad bowl.

3 Cut the apple into small pieces. Don't use the core of the apple. Add the apple pieces to the salad bowl.

4 **Chop** the pineapple slices into small pieces and add them to the salad bowl.

5 **Peel** the banana, then chop it into slices and add these to the bowl.

6 Peel the orange and divide it into segments. Add these to the salad.

7 In a small bowl, mix the lemon juice and the oil. Pour this mixture over the salad as a **dressing**.

8 Mix, or **toss**, the salad well just before you serve it.

Rice Pudding

Rice pudding is made in many different countries. This fruity Mexican version is very easy to make. There are two different sorts of rice—long and short grain. This dish works best with short-grain rice.

What you need

- ¼ cup rice
- ½ cup water
- 1 cup milk
- ½ cup granulated sugar
- ¼ cup raisins
- ½ tsp cinnamon
- 1 tbsp butter

What you do

 Put the rice into a saucepan and add the water. Bring it to a **boil**, then turn the heat down to low.

 Cover the pan and **simmer** for about 20 minutes, until the rice has soaked up all the water and is soft.

 Add the milk, sugar, raisins, and cinnamon to the pan, and stir everything together.

 Cook the rice pudding over low heat, stirring all the time, until all the milk has been soaked up. This should take about five minutes.

5 Stir the butter into the hot rice pudding until it **melts**, then serve.

ADDED EXTRAS

This rice pudding tastes really good served with fruit. You could try arranging a few segments of orange or some slices of apple alongside the rice pudding when you serve it.

Cinnamon Oranges

Many Mexican farmers grow oranges. This refreshing dessert is very easy to make.

What you need

2 oranges
2 tbsp granulated sugar
¼ tsp ground cinnamon

What you do

 Peel the skin from the oranges, then **slice** them thinly.

 Place the oranges in a serving bowl.

3 Mix the sugar and the cinnamon together in a small bowl, then **sprinkle** them over the oranges.

 Put the oranges, sugar, and cinnamon in the refrigerator for at least one hour before serving, to **chill** them.

MEXICAN DESSERTS

Desserts and other sweet things are very popular in Mexico. Some of the most popular desserts are made from fresh fruit, often served with spices and sugar or honey, as in this dish.

Ready to eat: 1 hour 15 minutes (including 1 hour to chill the oranges). Difficulty: *. Serves 2.

MEXICAN MARKETS

Many Mexican people buy their fruits and vegetables from street markets. Most Mexican towns have a market day, or *dia del mercado*. Markets are a good place not only to shop, but also to meet people.

Caramel Custard

A version of caramel custard is made in many countries around the world. In Mexico, this dish is called *flan*. It was probably brought to Mexico by the Spanish conquerors in the 16th century, and it is still a favorite today. This dish needs time to **chill** in the refrigerator, so make it several hours before you want to eat it.

What You need

2 eggs

⅓ cup granulated sugar

1 tbsp water

1 cup 2 percent milk

¼ tsp vanilla extract

What You do

1 **Preheat** the oven to 300°F (150°C).

2 Crack the eggs into a bowl. **Beat** them with a fork or a whisk until the yolk and the white are mixed.

3 Put half the sugar into a saucepan and add the water. Put the saucepan over low heat and stir gently until all the sugar has **dissolved**.

 4 Turn up the heat and **boil** quickly, without stirring, until the mixture turns golden. Pour this **syrup** into one or two small ramekins or ovenproof dishes.

5 Heat the milk in a saucepan over medium heat. Add the rest of the sugar and the vanilla **extract**. Heat for another three minutes, until the sugar has dissolved.

6 Let the milk **cool** down slightly, then stir the beaten eggs into it. Pour the mixture on top of the syrup and put the ramekins into a large, ovenproof dish. Carefully pour hot water around them until the water reaches about halfway up their sides.

7 **Cover** the ovenproof dish with foil, then put it in the oven and **bake** for 45 minutes.

8 Take the ovenproof dish out of the oven. Lift the hot ramekins of custard out of the ovenproof dish.

9 Leave the custard to cool, then put it into the refrigerator for at least three hours.

10 Dip the bottom of the ramekins into hot water to loosen the custard. Run a knife around the edge of the ramekins.

11 Quickly turn the custard out onto a plate before serving.

Mexican Hot Chocolate

The combination of plain chocolate, cinnamon, and vanilla is typically Mexican. In fact, Mexican chocolate bars often have cinnamon and vanilla already added to them.

What you need

4½ oz. plain chocolate, broken into chunks

1½ cups water

2 cups milk

½ tsp ground cinnamon

¼ tsp vanilla extract

What you do

 1 You will either need a heatproof bowl that fits on top of your saucepan, or you can **melt** the chocolate in the microwave, in a non-metallic, microwave-proof bowl.

 2 Break the chocolate into pieces and put it into your bowl. Then follow either step 3a or step 3b.

 3a Put the water into a saucepan. Heat it over medium heat until just bubbling at the edges, but not **boiling**. Reduce the heat to low. Put the bowl of chocolate on top and leave until melted (about five minutes).

 3b Alternatively, cook the chocolate on medium power in the microwave for 1 minute and 20 seconds and stir until melted.

 4 Warm the milk in a small saucepan. Slowly stir half the milk into the melted chocolate.

5 Pour the chocolate mixture back into the saucepan with the rest of the milk. Stir in the cinnamon and vanilla **extract**. Heat for a few more minutes.

6 Pour the hot chocolate into cups.

COLD CHOCOLATE

You can also use this recipe to make a cold chocolate drink. Leave the hot chocolate to cool, then **whisk** it with a fork or whisk before pouring it into cups.

BREAKFAST BREAD

Hot chocolate is often drunk for breakfast in Mexico. It is sometimes accompanied by *pan de yema*, a type of bread cooked in egg yolks that is dipped into the hot chocolate.

Further Information

Here are some places to find out more about Mexico and Mexican cooking.

Books

Coronado, Rosa. *Cooking the Mexican Way* (*Easy Menu Ethnic Cookbooks*). Minneapolis: Lerner, 2009.

Fauchald, Nick. *Funky Chicken Enchiladas: And Other Mexican Dishes*. Minneapolis: Picture Window, 2009.

Locricchio, Matthew. *The Second International Cookbook for Kids*. Tarrytown, NY: Marshall Cavendish, 2008.

Sheen, Barbara. *Foods of Mexico* (*A Taste of Culture*). Detroit: KidHaven, 2005.

Ward, Karen. *The Young Chef's Mexican Cookbook*. New York: Crabtree, 2001.

Websites

www.dltk-kids.com/recipesdb/viewbycourse.asp?cid=13

http://kids-cooking.suite101.com/article.cfm/mexican_recipes_kids_can_make

www.circletimekids.com/WorldLibrary/countries/Mexico/recipes

www.kids-cooking-activities.com/Mexican-cooking.html

Healthy Eating

This diagram shows the types and proportion of food you should eat to stay healthy. Eat plenty of foods from the *grains* group and plenty from the *fruits* and *vegetables* groups. Eat some foods from the *milk* group and the *meat and beans* group. Foods from the *oils* group are not necessary for a healthy diet, so eat these in small amounts or only occasionally.

Mexican cooking uses many ingredients from the two largest food groups. Rice and tortillas are from the grains group. People also eat lots of different kinds of vegetables and beans, so you can see how healthy Mexican cooking is!

↑ The MyPyramid food pyramid shows the proportion of food from each food group you should eat to achieve a healthy, balanced diet. This takes into account everything you eat, including snacks.

Glossary

bake cook something in the oven

beat mix something together strongly using a fork, spoon, or whisk

blend mix ingredients together in a blender or food processor

boil cook a liquid on the stove top. Boiling liquid bubbles and steams strongly.

broil cook by being exposed to direct heat

carbohydrate food (such as a potato) that contains sugar and starch, which give us energy

chill put something in the refrigerator to make it cold before serving it

chop cut something into pieces using a knife

colander bowl-shaped container with holes in it, used for draining vegetables and straining

cool allow hot food to become cold. You should always allow food to cool before putting it in the refrigerator.

cover put a lid on a pan, or foil over a dish

dissolve mix something into a liquid until it disappears

dough soft mixture of flour and liquid that sticks together and can be shaped or rolled out

drain remove liquid, usually by pouring something into a colander or sieve

dressing oil and vinegar sauce for salad

empire large area ruled by an emperor

extract very strong flavoring, such as vanilla or almond extract

flake break something, such as a piece of fish, into small pieces

fry cook something in oil in a pan

garnish decorate food—for example, with fresh herbs or lemon wedges

grate break something, such as cheese, into small pieces using a grater

grease rub fat over a surface to stop food from sticking to it

knead keep pressing and pushing dough with your hands so that it becomes very soft and stretches easily

mash crush something, such as a potato, until it is soft and pulpy

melt change from solid to liquid when heated

monsoon tropical storm

nomadic lifestyle in which people move frequently to find food

nourishing good for our bodies and our health

peel remove the skin of a fruit or vegetable

preheat turn on the oven or broiler in advance, so that it is hot when you are ready to use it

protein body-building material found in some foods, such as beans, eggs, and meat

shred cut or tear something, such as lettuce, into small pieces

simmer cook a liquid on the stove top. Simmering liquid bubbles and steams gently.

slice cut something into thin, flat pieces

sprinkle scatter small pieces or drops onto something

syrup thick, sweet liquid made from sugar and water

thaw defrost something that has been frozen

toss turn the leaves in a salad over a few times so they are coated in dressing

tropical hot, wet climate

vegetarian food that does not contain meat or fish. People who do not eat meat or fish are called vegetarians.

vitamin natural chemical in food that the body uses to stay healthy

Index

accompaniments
>> corn bread 16
>> savory fruit salad 34
>> tortillas 12
avocados 8
>> guacamole 14
bean and potato patties 24
beans 8
>> bean and potato patties 24
>> chili con carne 28
broiled corn on the cob
>> with salsa 20
caramel custard 40
cheese-filled enchiladas 22
chili con carne 28
chilies 6, 7, 8, 9
>> broiled corn on the cob
>>> with salsa 20
>> chili con carne 28
>> fish burritos 30
>> Mexican rice 32
>> picadillo 26
chocolate 7, 8, 9
>> Mexican hot chocolate 42
cinnamon oranges 38
corn bread 16
corn soup 18
desserts
>> caramel custard 40
>> cinnamon oranges 38
>> rice pudding 36
drinks
>> Mexican hot chocolate 42
fish burritos 30

guacamole 14
main courses
>> bean and potato patties 24
>> cheese-filled enchiladas 22
>> chili con carne 28
>> fish burritos 30
>> Mexican rice 32
>> picadillo 26
Mexican hot chocolate 42
Mexican rice 32
picadillo 26
rice pudding 36
savory fruit salad 34
starters and snacks
>> broiled corn on the cob
>>> with salsa 20
>> corn soup 18
>> guacamole 14
>> tortillas 12
sweet corn 4, 8, 9
>> broiled corn on the cob
>>> with salsa 20
>> corn soup 18
tomatoes 6, 7, 9
>> broiled corn on the cob
>>> with salsa 20
>> cheese-filled enchiladas 22
>> chili con carne 28
>> Mexican rice 32
>> picadillo 26
tortillas 6, 7, 9, 12